# MITROPOULOS AND THE
# NORTH HIGH BAND

## Also by Brenda Ueland

**IF YOU WANT TO WRITE**

**ME**

The above titles, originally published by G.P. Putnam's Sons,
New York in 1938 and 1939, were re-published in 1983 by:

**The Schubert Club**
**302 Landmark Center**
**St. Paul, Minnesota 55102**

Brenda Ueland

# MITROPOULOS AND THE
# NORTH HIGH BAND

### AND OTHER PIECES ON MUSICAL LIFE
### BY
# Brenda Ueland

MANUFACTURED IN THE UNITED STATES OF AMERICA

Printed by

*Colwell/North Central, inc., St. Paul, Minnesota*

ISBN 0-912373-03-2

# CHAPTERS

# INTRODUCTION

I first met Brenda Ueland several years ago by a blazing fireplace in her house by Lake Harriet. She looked a bit like photographs of Liszt in the Rome years. "There are seven great women — all actresses" she told me. As I was leaving she said, "Get your daughter a job as an usher at the Guthrie."

We have since become close friends. I've visited her many times and her conversation is spirited. She recently suggested that a good prayer would be "for jovial courage and a light heart." "Did you know that the Sioux Indian word for generosity is the same as for courage?" she added.

We often talk about music. With wild admiration she has spoken many times of the great musician Dmitri Mitropoulos, conductor of the Minneapolis Symphony Orchestra from 1937 to 1949. John K. Sherman wrote in his history of the orchestra, *Maestros and Musicians*, that Mitropoulos "sold his soul to music and conducted the orchestra like a man possessed." A perfect match for Brenda, I thought to myself, when I read Sherman's opinion. Mitropoulos, of course, played the familiar classics but, Sherman reported, he also "rarely resisted the temptation to present new works" and in fact made the Twin Cities international capitals of contemporary music.

Brenda Ueland loved Mitropoulos and attended his (and many other) concerts. Her impressions bring to life a brilliant period of music-making several decades ago. They have been gathered together in this little book from newspaper columns she wrote, her diaries, and her autobiography *Me*.

*Mitropoulos and the North High Band* is not music criticism. It is descriptive writing about music from within a culture — the deeply felt response of a listener filled with sophisticated wonder. An audience is a mysterious part of a performance. You don't usually know what it's doing. Brenda Ueland's vivid prose articulates what's in the audience's heart.

> — *Bruce Carlson, Executive Director*
> *The Schubert Club*
> *April, 1984*

I have a theory that music lifts the spirit from the ground to a little freedom. It is as though you float a little above yourself, and dust falls away, and what we are meant to be is there. Jacob Boehme said that Eternity is that flash of time when we are what we love. And music does that — "The bright shoots of everlastingness."

— *Brenda Ueland*

# I

The first rehearsal of the Symphony and Sam Grodnick let us in. The auditorium is all dim and dark and on the stage are the orchestra players, the old friends: nice ruddy Mr. Koch with his cello, Spanish-looking Mr. Messeas, strong young Mr. Heiderich with his straight profile, Karl Scheurer, etc.

"What are they playing now?" we whispered to each other. Such lovely music and it had that 18th century way of ending a bar. "Bach?" No. And as they practiced and repracticed — "Brahms?" Yes, like Brahms because the chords are so rich and melodious, opulent and prismatic like rainbows. "Oh," we whispered, "they're playing the Brahms *Variations on a Theme of Haydn*. Of course. They will play it Friday night."

Mitropoulos wore a light blue sweater, his shoulders powerful and relaxed. ("He is a faun on Mt. Olympus . . . And like Savanarola," we whispered.) He is before them without music score or baton. And he is happy because he is working again (he is devoured by jackals and hyenas when he isn't) and he cannot keep from

shining smiles of happiness like a child when
Christmas is imminent. And he can't keep the
love out of his voice, the inclusive feeling he has
for them all, almost as though he were the father
of adorable children.

Now you would think it would be a time
of tension. Well, there is immense inner excitement, but his voice is all goodness and joy.
"Again!" he says. "Go back to N and start
from the fifth measure before this place." (He
has no music yet he knows where N is.) Then
he lifts his hands and they play. "No." He drops
his hands and they trail to a stop — tootle —
tootle — detoot. (And how I love the tuning up
of the orchestra, the delicate springlets of sound
running every which way.)

Now this is the bliss of being at rehearsals: sitting in the darkness, you begin to hear
it through HIMSELF. You lean forward into
the lucent cloud of music, and, listening, you
begin to hear all the streams of it, winding in
and out. You hear how he is working definition
out of chaos. The violins more clear and more
debonair, he wants them, more casual and light-
hearted.

"You see it is —" and he sings it —
"da-da-DA!" And he not only sings it but he
dances it. How his hands, his very self, can

show everything is just extraordinary. ("I think
they are so wrong," we whisper in the darkness,
"to say he doesn't need to use his body so
much. Why it just IS the music." How utterly,
flabbergastingly extraordinary he is! What a
dancer "on yonder green hill-O.")

His arms fall limp. "No, I must hear
this flute." And then you hear it yourself —
the adorable flute singing through the lovely
cloud of song. Oh, that flute tune! Some
shepherds on a sleepy midsummer hill far away.

They play it all through. His face
lighted with joyful excitement (I see spokes
of rays in wheels around his head), he springs
down among the violins, pulling out their
theme, bounds to point with a fierce index
finger into the horns. To whip the rhythm
he leaps high, stamps his heels in pistol shots.
It makes the heart leap to see the terrific and
wild exaggeration of his rehearsals.

I have a theory that music lifts the
spirit from the ground to a little freedom. It
is as though you float a little above yourself,
and dust falls away, and what we are meant
to be is there. Jacob Boehme said that Eternity is that flash of time when we are what
we love. And music does that — "The bright
shoots of everlastingness."

And is that why the orchestra players' faces become so wonderful? Or is it that I am music-enchanted? Because it does the very same thing to chairs, walls. (When my sister used to play the piano in her house I said: "The furniture gets much prettier.")

The orchestra players look at Mitropoulos. No face smiles. Then they play again. And these everyday people (like the rest of us — in suits, wearing glasses, etc.) —every face becomes so serious and beautiful and somehow seraphic. It seems not to happen to jazz orchestras. But great music brings the alchemy.

— 1942

# II

So many people I know are taking music lessons — secretly and bashfully because they are entirely grown-up now and it seems a little queer to be fumblingly searching out the notes of "The Happy Farmer." But it is a wonderful thing to do. If I were a doctor I would prescribe for 90 percent of my patients: "Take music lessons."

When I was a child my music teacher was Mrs. Alexandra Hollander Fahnestock. First there was Miss Dillinger, who made us cry tears of exasperation. Then a Miss Olson who told us to make our hands like claws and hammer at Plaidy exercises, the most uphill, tiresome, impossible thing. My sister got to play quite fancily and well Mendelssohn's *Songs Without Words* and Sinding's "Rustle of Spring." But I got nowhere.

But later by some chance I was sent to Mrs. Fahnestock. Well, she was a wonderful person. She was elderly, a Jewess with a dark dramatic head, hair elaborately coiffed and raised black eyebrows. Short hands, white and pulpy and covered with rings.

She lived very far away. I had to transfer twice on the streetcar to get there. It was a railroad apartment on Park Avenue and Twenty-Second Street. In the front room there was her grand piano and fringed portieres and plush hassocks, and the piano was bristling with standing photographs of European singers and virtuosi. She was a member of a distinguished musical family. Her brother was a famous Hollander in Berlin, a conductor of the Berlin Conservatory.

She was utterly adorable, dear, good, precious, fascinating, wonderful. Full of praise and thrilling musical excitement, of stories about Melba and Lucca, a prima donna, she told me, whose blue eyes were so heavily encircled with double-fringed eyelashes that in Germany the bakers called a certain cake "Lucca eyes." Mrs. Fahnestock told me that when she herself was young and walking down Unter den Linden, a passer-by was heard to say: "She looks like the Ninth Symphony." And this was the greatest compliment of her life.

She made me feel that she saw something special in me. And it was the same with all her pupils. I don't know how many years I took lessons. It seemed to me to go on forever. I think the family forgot about it. They just paid the very small bill, perhaps about $1.50 a lesson, as though it were the grocery bill. I was never catechized or pressed about practicing (there were seven children). And I never, as long as I took lessons, practiced enough, or at all. Through all my childhood I never once went to a lesson with that pleased inner peace: "I have really practiced this week. You will be surprised how I have polished off things this week!" Always uneasiness and bluff.

But Mrs. Fahnestock liked the way I thundered at the piano and had power in pieces that were slow. Chords. That slow Prelude by Chopin. Oh, I could do those and put in expression!

And not only did she not reprove me but she fed me. Perhaps that is what kept me going to my lessons.

I think she fed me because she was an angel of German-Jewess hospitality. I would arrive there after high school. We walked the length of the dark railroad apartment to the dining room with a window on some dim backyard. She brewed tea (we were not allowed to have tea at home, a stimulant!) and she gave me wonderful fat doughnuts doused in white powdered sugar.

Then to the piano. She sat beside me fingering a long gold chain with large topaz-colored beads on it. I sat down with misgivings and played, with bluff and vehemence, something from Schumann's *Albums of Childhood.* She expounded it. It was a story, she said. "You see he tells a wonderful story. These arpeggios —he plucks the harp as he tells it . . . "

Well, bless Mrs. Fahnestock! All those years of lessons, I at least learned to read music and soaked in an affection for it, and now after so many years if I start to play at 11 o'clock at night, feeling tired and pinched, I will still be there at one o'clock or later, an entirely different person, alive and transfigured. That is what music does.

Mrs. Fahnestock —so grand, so cultured, so distinguished. I think they were quite poor, hard-up and pinched. She was married to Mr. Fahnestock, very tall, elegant, with a very large nose like a statesman. He was a floorwalker at the New Englander and she had a son, Noel, distant, unsmiling and mysterious. I had and still have an anxious sad feeling they did not like her very much.

— 1948

# III

Fritz Kreisler played the Beethoven
Concerto at the Symphony and I suppose that
is as close to Heaven as a concert-goer gets.
The soldierly handsome Kreisler has lived
through two wars. He is over 70. His father
was a compassionate Viennese doctor with a
huge practice among the very poor. Kreisler
fought in the war of 1914 and was nearly
killed, but a Cossack's lifted saber got tangled
in some gear and he was picked up half dead
out of a Lemberg trench. America was not at
war so he came here and gave concerts and
was adored, as he is now. He was criticized
as an Austrian soldier pulling in American
money! So he told why he did it. He said he
sent the money back to Vienna to the families
of French, Russian, American musicians who
were stranded there, and he said: "To keep up
the requirements of these forty people took
the major portion of my salary. It is not pleas-
ant for me to tell of the things I am privileged
to do for others."

"I am privileged —" That is just like
him, just the way he would describe it. They

say that he has supported in his life more than
a thousand people.

Kreisler was robust, athletic, almost
military.  He swam, rode horseback.  He had
colossal health.  He was fascinated by books,
by all the great economic changes in the world.
He liked sports, politics.

He said: "The simpler and freer from
ostentation the life of an artist is the more
beautiful his playing will be."

He said: "An artist should marry young
and if he does not marry young he should
marry anyway.  It is absolutely only the right
way for an artist to live, as it is probably for
anybody."

An English critic once said: "Kreisler
is a supreme artist and supremely popular.
This is an unbelievable paradox."  Because the
Art-For-Art's sake people say that the moment
an artist takes notice of what other people
want and tries to supply it, he ceases to be an
artist.  They hold that Art should never be popular, but that the public should try to make itself artistic.

Actually, of course, the public is always
trying to make itself artistic.  With an almost
pathetic patience it listens to music it cannot
really hear, looks at pictures it cannot really

see. (Chesterton defined a yawn as a "silent yell.")
A young French writer once said that the public should give an artist "serious, patient attention." Anatole France answered promptly that
this was "a grievous maxim. The more I see
the more I feel nothing except what is easy is
beautiful." And Kreisler, like Anatole France,
believes the true artist will avoid causing the
least trouble for his listeners. (That's just what
I think.) He does not exact  attention, he sur-
prises it.

His music has something that I can only
describe as "coherence." When he plays you
know what is coming, and what has vanished
is all connected with it.

Deems Taylor wrote in 1935: "For
once I am on the side of the public that puts
the violinist first and the music second. No
one but Kreisler gives me such a feeling of being
in communion with a great spirit. It springs
from his unselfishness — " Yes. Just the way
he stands there while the orchestra begins, and
looks up, his violin hanging in one hand, listening to the orchestra — so unpretentious. He
seems actually to care about us, the audience.

At Friday's concert there was a young
man in front of me and he had black hair and
spectacles. And when Kreisler came on, with

what wild vehemence he started to stand up.
He looked around at the 5,000 people in the
audience. At me — "You must stand up!" he
seemed to say.

Well we didn't. We didn't have the self-
respect and courage. So he stayed there,
moving up and down, half-crouched, express-
ing everything I felt: "Damn it, here is one of
the greatest men alive, treading this miserable
earth at this moment. You must stand up!"

I'm grateful for that fine young man
who knows what Kreisler is and deserves.

— 1946

# IV

Paul Robeson is coming to sing on Sunday for Mrs. Carlyle Scott's huge concert. When I saw him (and my beautiful daughter wanted to go too) he was playing chess solitaire in his room in the Nicollet Hotel. He is just monstrous, huge, his shoulders so broad and mighty you cannot guess his height. I look it up now and find it is six feet three. His face is black, his eyes wide apart — and they have an energy and glare like the statue of Don Juan come to life. And once in a while he will smile and it is like the sun coming out, and, seeing that perfect arch of teeth, you think: "No wonder he sings like that!"

He told me he has a passion for the study of phonetics (he speaks Russian, French, German, Italian, Spanish and reads more than 20 languages including Gaelic and Chinese), and at first when he talked to us in the interview, he spoke with the most distinguished, scholarly inflection and accent, so that I thought of a Harvard professor — I imagined that Chief Justice Oliver Wendell Holmes would talk just that way. But presently as he

seemed to trust us and to like us a little bit,
behold, he talked in an entirely different voice,
his own childhood Negro dialect, far more
musical, warmer, more full of imagery than
the other.

I remember that we asked him about
how white people treated him. He was very
benignant and kind and spoke of it without
a tincture of antagonism, only thoughtfully.
And he said (and it is the experience of all
colored people) that sometimes white people
would want to make a great fuss about him,
do fine things for him, "take him up," and
they would be very hearty and unctuous
about it, but underneath there was the invisible patronizing — that subtle invisible thing —
as though they were saying to themselves,
"See how fine I am, and how I encourage a
member of the Negro race, yes, indeed!" It
is very subtle and delicate but he can tell it at
once. "And I don't allow it, I don't allow
them to know me."

I asked him then what could be done
for Negroes. He said that as the United
Nations grew stronger "and it is found that
500 million Chinese cannot be kicked around
and 400 million Indians and 150 million
Africans, why then 13 million American

Negroes can't be kicked around. As for myself, I have always felt proud of being a
Negro. I have never had one second of feeling any other way."

He is 48. His father was a preacher in
Princeton, New Jersey, and he went to Rutgers.
He was the class valedictorian, a Phi Beta Kappa.
He was Walter Camp's choice for All-American
football end. He studied law at Columbia.
Then Eugene O'Neill asked him to be in
*Emperor Jones*, and here they discovered his
voice. In the part where Emperor Jones is lost
in the jungle, he is supposed to whistle to keep
up his spirits, but Robeson's whistling was not
any good at all. So they decided he should
sing a spiritual instead. The effect? He found
himself famous as both a singer and an actor.
In London he has played Othello opposite
Mrs. Patrick Campbell.

At the Symphony concert Robeson
sang the death scene from *Boris Godunov*
by Mussorgsky, and I think it is because
Pushkin wrote the great drama. Pushkin, who
is Byron and Shakespeare combined to the
Russians, was a fiery officer who died in a
duel at 37, a great poet, a great genius. His
heroine Tatiana in *Eugene Onegin* was the
forerunner of the great heroines of Tolstoy and

Dostoevsky, and she represents a far greater conception of Woman than was to be found in English literature. Pushkin had curly hair, a dark face and a fierce generous heart. His great-grandfather was Hannibal, a Negro prince at the court of Peter the Great.

Once when Robeson was a boy in the sixth grade he brought home a report card with seven As and one B. It was the best record of the class. "Son, what's that B doing there?" asked his father. He adored his father and never forgot the incident. "Nothing less than perfection" became his watchword. And so it is now.

— 1946

# V

In the afternoon Maria Montana sang at the College Women's Club. She was born in Montana and studied in Italy so she took the Italian-sounding name. It is just right for a very Americanissimo prima donna from Montana.

And Mitropoulos played her accompaniment. The person who introduced him told how he had been given a doctor's degree at the University. "Dr. Mitropoulos . . " she said; "Dr. Mitropoulos will say a few words to us." (Will they call him that all the time? It is like saying "Dr. Galahad.")

He arose from the piano in his easy way. He said he did not like to stand on the little platform. "If I had some chair I could sit on. . . " So they handed him one and he stood behind it, lifted and twirled it, and it became a light stick in his very strong hands.

"I have not prepared anything because I have better things to do than to make speeches, I think. And I have worked very hard this morning, a rehearsal. And some things have not gone well. On most days at two o'clock I take a little nap but today I will try to talk to you." And up to this point I think he had not decided what he was going to say.

"I suppose I can tell you about the Orchestra," and he started to tell of their concert tour. "As you know, we go because the Symphony needs money. A tour makes $19,000 after the traveling expenses are paid, and to make this money it is necessary to have a concert every day. In six weeks, we played 40 concerts." (An aghast sigh from us all.)

He was talking quietly in his very deep tranquil voice. And then he said: "I cannot tell you how absolutely terrible is the hardship of this tour! Packed in the train like sardines —" (I think this was his metaphor.) "To arrive in a town at 5 o'clock. Then a concert. In some places we were late. Once the people had been waiting for us since 8:30. We began the concert at 10:30. The hotels often had no rooms so the boys had to to sleep in the lobby or on the floor. The food — it is impossible to get any good food at all. And never at the right time. I conducted many times without food, though I do not care. But the boys who play the

wind instruments must eat an hour and a
half before they play. So we arrived in some
towns too late for them to eat. And after
the concert there is no eating place open.
And up at six — impossible to get breakfast
then — in this fatigue and hunger, then they
are supposed to play and give their soul."

Gentle and good and patient Mitropoulos
— talking along in such a subdued way, but more
and more he was bursting with indignation about
"the boys."

"In every town we left men in the hospital. Many cases of pneumonia. In Quebec,
you know how it goes up and down —" (gestur-
ing) — "a place for skis. And twenty below zero.
Well, one of our first violinists made himself into
a ski and broke his arm. And this not only keeps
him out of the Orchestra, but he cannot work
now on other jobs that he has. You see the boys
must have these jobs because they don't make
enough money from the Orchestra.

"For me it is all right. I did not take
sick. But this just made it possible for me to
suffer morally even more. And I am the conductor. I have attention and praise and triumph.
They do not.

"And on top of this, the money allowed
them for expenses was not enough. So they had

to appeal to their Union. A dollar a day was asked, but in bargaining they were given fifty cents." And the niggardliness and fretfulness of all this appalled him and drove him to a mighty anger.

And that they had to ASK for it! That anybody should ever have to ask for what is just! "The budget, people say . . . Business . . ." Like all great men Mitropoulos is horrified and unbelieving that people do not see any values beyond the budgets and beyond the neat numerals on paper and beyond the cold-hearted haggling of a labor-and-business policy.

This is the way he puts it: "It is always 'the little man' who gets pinched, tweaked, misused. We" — he meant the budget and business people and the fine audiences at concerts and even magnificent conductors like himself — "We always take it out on the ordinary person, 'the little man.' "

Then he told us we must pay the Orchestra decently or not have it. The men get the lowest salaries in the country. They are continually being urged to go to other cities.

"And if we raise the price of seats," he said to us reproachfully, "you won't go to the concerts." And so we could only gaze back at him in mum, doleful guilt. (Though everybody wanted to say, "Of course we will!")

Well, he looked out of his extraordinary ram-colored eyes, full of pale fire, and sadly sighed and said: "I have talked enough. Now we'll make some music." And he went back to the piano.

Maria Montana came back and sang lovely, perfect songs by Rachmaninoff and French songs with words by Verlaine. Mitropoulos put on his glasses and played them beautifully and humbly.

— 1945

# VI

January 14th, 1937. Thursday.
Harriet and I went to hear Enesco the violinist
— a Schubert Club concert at the Peoples
Church Auditorium. This is a wonderful experience. He is medium height, his black hair
parted in the middle and growing thickly all
over his head like that of a very young person.
A small lock on the right would fall an inch over
his forehead after long playing. He has a pale
puffy face, is fifty or sixty. His face is noble
and handsome, a dark Roman face except that
his nose is more delicate and narrower than
Caesar's. His eyelids are puffed up and faintly
bluish, and when he plays I think that some of
the time his eyes are shut, though he has not
then the foolish look that most people have
when their eyes are shut. You think they
might be open like the eyes of an Egyptian
statue. His face is in general like Napoleon's
but it is noble, romantic and sad. I cannot bear
Napoleon's face when he was either young or
old. (Though I am supposed to look like him.)
He has dumpy narrow shoulders, almost shoul-
derless like a bird, and not a small waist, and he

walks oddly with picked womanish steps and toeing out. He does not stand on his feet well, but the weight is behind the balls of his feet. Then he begins to play. His left hand is sallow and unbelievably delicate and soft. Slender, tremulous fingers.

He played first a Mozart, then a Paganini, resolute and triumphant and strong. Then the "Fountain of Arethuse." I never heard before this a fountain in music — the muted lovely dissonant notes falling like jewels, like rhinestones, always a little off key but always musical and coherent and understandable so that you hear every note with rapt attention. And such pianissimo! (he puts on the muted bridge often), you can barely hear it: it is dry October leaves rustling, the faintest and most beautiful sounds. Sometimes he bends his head low and you feel that he knows more than anyone in the world, that he is 5000 years old, a gypsy, an Egyptian perhaps.

Afterwards I ask Frances Boardman about him. She says he is the sweetest, the most unspoiled, the humblest, simplest person in the whole world. His accompanist says that, who has been with him for years: just adores him, says there is no one so good, so patient, so unassuming.

Friday, January 15, 1937. To hear Rachmaninoff at the Symphony. He comes in tall and lank like a stork or crane, moves so slowly that he seems feeble, almost with the languid indifference of a drunken man. He puts his loose-kneed long leg forward to take a short step and in his lassitude it almost swings behind, as though, like a very weak old man, he were to retreat rather than progress. But his playing is full of power and beauty, of singing and talking. It is indescribably different, superior to all other pianists. It is the difference between a man and an angel.

A Miss Blanche Humpus-Dumpus Johnson (not her real name) made a speech during intermission (a purple dress, a pink corsage and white hair). A very nice woman but the longest, most cumbersome, boring, platitudinous speech I have ever heard.

"The boys and girls of the public schools of the City of Minneapolis and, frankly, too, of St. Paul, know the thrill that comes from the music of the Minneapolis Symphony Orchestra, and it gives these boys and girls of the public schools that opportunity to experience, I may say, themselves, to actually be present at and to hear the music of these members of the Minneapolis Symphony who with their splendid efforts do this for our young people, for our boys and girls of our two cities, both Minneapolis and St. Paul, and not only for our boys and girls of our high schools but also of our grade schools, for music; and by music I mean the BEST music becomes a factor that can and should come intó the lives not only of older people but of boys and girls in the lower grades and even, if I may say so, of the kindergarten system of our civic life."

Rolf says as we get into the car in the underground garage: "I talked extra long and cordially to Virginia Rice because I saw Carl T. Peebles about to pounce and button-hole me."

I say: "I may hire him to follow you around so that you will be nice to ladies."

Wonderful Virginia R. with her narrowed smiling blue eyes  said: "I used to believe that God and the angels could see everything I did. But then I got to doing things I didn't want them to see so I didn't believe in them any more."

— 1937

# VII

Mitropoulos comes on and just from his easy fluent stride you can tell his music will be better than any other's. He faces us for the Star Spangled Banner, keeping time with thumb and forefinger once in a while and a little vibrant, whirl of his fist. He always stands very straight, looking up, and you can tell what he is thinking about when he plays it: about Greece and this country, and about U.S. tanks near Bastogne. And he is thinking what the words mean: "Land of the Free and Brave." I think those are the two very best adjectives in our language. Sometimes we sing the Star Spangled Banner with just an absent-minded waw-waw-waw, but with Mitropoulos we sing it in a clear voice and it comes out seriously from the heart.

Schnabel was the soloist. He played a Beethoven concerto. He is the greatest Beethoven scholar of all time, they say. But then the Orchestra played his own First Symphony, the first time it has ever been performed. To me it seemed strikingly ugly. It was as though he were continuously saying to us, "Now wait. I can make it even uglier than this."

There was one musical "ping!" that fluttered in the air several measures in the third movement, the only pretty sound in the whole thing, and it tinkled sweetly out of the celeste.

I am sure that mathematically, in terms of an immense intellect and decades of scholarship, that if one were musically erudite enough to see into such a thing, his Symphony would fill one with the deepest awed admiration, like an Einstein formula. But where is the beauty, the poetry, the music, the dulcet tender voices, the singing, the lyricalness, the nightingales, the wind, the music of the spheres that the constellations of the stars make wheeling in their orbits and that only the ancients could hear when the world was quiet and there was nothing louder in this planet than a blacksmith shop?

David Shearer said, grinning when we encountered him in the garage under the Adult Education Building: "But surely life is not THAT bad!" Because they say that to us when we dare not to like modern music: "Modern music is just an expression of our modern age." As though that alone made it a work of art.

There is a long walk through the tunnel to the underground garage, and at the entrance of the tunnel there is another tunnel that branches off and disappears into mysterious jail-like darkness, and sometimes there is emitted from thence a mechanical wheezing and strangling as though a bull-dozer were being killed by a five-ton, worm-gear dump truck. Mr. George Leonard, jocularly to David Shearer: "Is that the Fifth Movement of the Schnabel?"

They tell me that a century hence I will be proved a fool and a Philistine and a most bigoted old fogey and they say that Schoenberg and Schnabel and the others are the Bachs and Beethovens of our day. No so. Beauty is eternal and the Lord.

— 1944

# VIII

Joseph Wechsberg (in a charming book, *Looking For a Bluebird*) tells of hired claques at the opera. There was a permanent claque at the Metropolitan when Gatti-Casazza was director. At the Warsaw opera once Artur Rodzinski acted as claque chief. "And there was nothing disgraceful about the claque at the Vienna Staatsoper where I had the honor of belonging in the middle twenties."

It consisted of about forty insolvent students who loved good opera. They were given a free ticket to standing room and their claque chief was Schostal. "I met him one night in the Peterskeller, across from the Staatsoper and frequented by night chauffeurs and bums. Schostal moved over to the piano and hammered out a few bars of *Salome, Fledermaus,* etc. After each I had to tell the act and scene from which it came. 'All right,' he said, 'we'll try him at *Tristan* next Saturday' — because *Tristan* was fairly easy to begin since the claque worked only at the end of each act."

But a claquer's nightmare was *Carmen.* "You start working right after Carmen's gypsy

song, and you applaud after her dance with the
castanets. Then Escamillo enters (applause) and
leaves (more applause).

"Schostal could feel whether the aria was
going over or not. A claquer's most unpardonable
crime is to start applause which is not taken up
by the public and perhaps is even drowned out
by outraged hisses. Schostal seldom made a mistake.

"He himself never applauded during a
performance — generals do not shoot rifles —
but at the end of an exceptionally good one he
would step down to the breastwork and benevo-
lently clap his hands for the stars. They never
failed to look up and give him a smile.

"He detested high pressure methods:
'We will not impose applause on the public.
We stimulate them and give them the clue at
the right time, and they take care of the rest.' "

The claque got only the free tickets,
though Schostal had fees from the singers:
"But this seemed fair enough. They all knew
he was incorruptible and never took money
from singers who were not good enough for
special applause."

Once the ambitious wife of a "big shot"
manufacturer was to sing *Tosca*. The tycoon,
who was a power behind the opera, sent for

Schostal and offered him money. "Sorry," he said, "Madame is not good enough for a Staatsoper." The furious husband bought up hundreds of seats and distributed them to his friends, but the result was disastrous.

They applauded at the wrong moments and the enraged public started hissing. From his seat Schostal watched the tragedy with grim satisfaction. Madame was through forever.

When Clemens Krauss became director of the Staatsoper, he publicly threatened to "rub out the claque." Schostal took up the challenge. The following evening Krauss conducted *Don Giovanni.* Schostal bought 30 expensive orchestra seats which he distributed "among those of us who owned tuxedos."

"When Krauss entered, we started a terrific ovation. During the intermission Schostal asked Krauss how he liked our work. 'Don't be ridiculous,' Krauss said, 'the applause was made by my admirers. Since when do you boys sit in the orchestra seats?'

"During the second act we applauded too early in Don Giovanni's "Deh viene" and started several 'wild' salvos. After the cemetery scene several of our boys shouted 'Bravo, Walter!' and when told by kindly neighbors that Krauss, not Bruno Walter, was conducting, they looked dumbfounded and unhappy.  The newspapers played up the story the next day and for weeks Krauss was greeted by malicious friends with, 'Bravo, Walter!'  After that he did not object to the claque any more."

— 1950

# IX

We drove to North High along Fremont
Avenue under the dim Gothic arches of the elm
trees. The North High band was giving a concert with the St. Cloud Technical High band.

The North High band filled the big stage,
boys and girls in their handsome uniforms with
ropes looped grandly on their shoulders, like
field marshals. They played a long program,
with Clive Cleary directing them. Sam Haveson
executed a trumpet solo. Very good it all was.

Then, after the intermission, the St.
Cloud band filed on the stage with its conductor,
Erwin Hertz, another chunky young man with
glasses. And the St. Cloud band was very loud
and businesslike, too, and played tunes from
*Oklahoma* and marches — Br-r-oum-za-za! And
there was a violin solo by Pollyanna Peterson.

There came the final piece on the program. The St. Cloud band squeezed itself onto
part of the stage and the North High band filed
on again, and both bands were going to play together — perhaps 250 endearingly pretty kids,
girls with ambrosial curls piled under their chins,
and sixteen-year-old boys with piccolos. Then

Mr. Maass, the principal, led Mitropoulos up on the stage. "Mitropoulos of our Minneapolis Symphony has kindly consented to conduct one number . . . "

Well, Mitropoulos turned to all those highschool children and held up his hands. Nothing can describe it, the convulsive fire in the music now, the transfiguration! It was by Morton Gould and the air, "When Johnny Comes Marching Home" goes through it in drums and flutes and horns, dulcet and then dissonant and then loud as war itself. So triumphant and gay, martial and gay and bursting with happiness.

"Our boys will come marching home again!" the music was telling us. And we could see them and their brave jolly manhood, their quick marching up every Main Street in the country. Their smiles flashing at us under the flags. Their young might and hardihood that will build up the future. One shuddered and froze with pleasure, it was so beautiful and exciting.

You know how Mitropoulos conducts, the power in his hands. It is as though he alone forced and fired and galvanized them all, making every tootling highschool kid into a terrible great Mitropoulos himself. But there is no use in describing it, because I can't.

The audience was delighted and clapped loudly. One lone lady stood up staunchly and hoped to get them all to stand. To honor Mitropoulos. But the concert was over and the corridors filled with chatting kids and parents. I explored back of the stage. There alone in the dark was Mitropoulos walking up and down, head down, hands behind his back, lost in sadness. I could feel that. I guess one cannot have that genius for nothing, without exhaustion of spirit.

As I left the building I was pressed beside a girl clarinet-player from St. Cloud. "Are you having fun in Minneapolis?" "I'll say." "How many rehearsals did you have with Mitropoulos?" "One." "Was it a remarkable experience?" "I'll say." "Can you describe it? Why did you play for him so differently?"

She didn't know what I was talking about, relieved when other kids led her off to some icecream soda or juke box. Few people see what Mitropoulos is. Just as he lifts ordinary nice children into glory and a noble musicianship, that is what he does for Minneapolis, though we forget it. There is a star on his forehead and I can see it.

— 1945

Dimitri Mitropoulos

Mitropoulos

Fritz Kreisler

Hamline student Marie Guthrie with
Dimitri Mitropoulos and Ernst Krenek.

Lena Horne and Paul Robeson

Marian Anderson with Sol Hurok

Georges Enesco

Donald Ferguson

# X

There was the first concert of the
Friends of Chamber Music at the First Unita-
rian Church: Eva Knardahl and Robert Jamieson —both of the Symphony Orchestra and
two of our most dulcet and lovely virtuosi.
They played the piano and cello.

First Mr. Jamieson (young, fair, boy-
ish, limber) played Bach's Suite Number 4 in
E Flat Major For Unaccompanied Cello, one
of those Bach series of dances, an Allemand,
a Courante (a leaping dance; the word means
"running"), a Saraband (a grave, slow court
dance) and finally a Gigue (a jig.) It was an
excellent performance, and here I must say
how difficult, how impossible it is to convey
in speech the beauty, tenderness, gaiety,
gravity of the cello singing in Bach's noble
flowing notes.

After the intermission they played a
Debussy Sonata, Prologue and Serenade: mysterious and beautiful with sounds on cello
and piano as delicately muted as the sound of
water lapping the underside of a boat, and
sounds as tiny as the scratching of a dead leaf

on a tombstone. Although here I want to express a personal idiosyncrasy. Debussy, though so poetical and all, gives me a kind of uneasy hunger because he is so terribly irresolute, and it troubles me that he does not march anywhere. (I am a marcher.) How shall I describe it? It is like a very beautiful, very soft woman murmuring lovely sentences without a verb: never making a statement.

The final piece was a Brahms, and one's soul breathed again. "Yes, this is it!" one thought. "Here we are in the noble country! Here we are in the Elysian Fields!"

The audience was very large, the auditorium filled by thoughtful and attractive people. It is this writer's serious belief that Eva Knardahl plays the piano better than anyone in the world.

Alec Templeton played on Sunday in the Concert Bowl. He is Scottish, with a volatile face and dark fine eyes, but he cannot see through them because he was born blind. He learns by listening.

When he was to accompany Milstein in the Lalo concerto, he heard it once and then played it through with one mistake. He practices four hours in the afternoon, drinks nothing but ginger ale.

Sometime I will tell you why concert pianists don't drink. Not so much because drink eats away your liver and lights, but because you cannot possibly break through to any phenomenal skill; you can't make that leap, that mutation from the possible to the impossible.

At the Veteran's Hospital there was a dying young Negro soldier, a drummer, and there was one thing he had always wanted: green silk pyjamas. Two weeks before he died green silk pyjamas came from Kansas City. From Alec Templeton.

— 1961

# XI

The Paganini Quartet is at the Art Institute Wednesday, the second concert of the Twin Cities Chamber Music Society (i.e. Mrs. Staples, Mrs. Pflaum, Mrs. Hawks, Mrs. Zelle, Mrs. Carpenter, etc.). It is called Paganini because they play four Stradivarius instruments owned by Paganini himself. The viola is the very one for which Berlioz wrote *Harold in Italy* at Paganini's request. Stradivarius was 92 when he made the cello. And Mr. Temianka's violin, according to the expert, Emil Herrmann, is the very fiddle on which Paganini concertized for years.

Nicolo Paganini was the greatest violin virtuoso of all time. He even started the idea of virtuosity, that is to say, skill to the Nth power. He was born in Genoa in 1784, his father a gentleman in the shipping business and a clever musical amateur, and the thin, avid, black-haired little boy insisted, nagged, fretted to be taught. At 11 he was taken to Parma to take lessons of the famous Alessandro Rolla. Rolla heard him play and in astonishment said there was nothing he could teach him. So little Paganini went home, practiced alone. He would practice ten hours on a single passage. Presently he began to write his own compositions and made them so difficult that no one else could play them. He would give them to the best violinists, saying, "Try this," watch them stumble, get tangled in all strings, then take his own fiddle and sail through.

This was at the beginning of the nineteenth century, the most vaunting romantic epoch in all history — all nightingales, blowing hair, pistol duels, urns, weeping willows, noble revolutionaries. The young Napoleon was in Italy, and Byron, Shelley and Keats. Chopin was some place, and with George Sand. Garibaldi, with his lion's face and a golden mane, was a young sea captain.

Paganini made huge fees and threw the money away. He gambled and lost his violin. Then in Paris in 1831 he gave a concert and three great musical geniuses heard him and their future careers were immediately changed forever as though by a violent chemical action.

At the concert was Liszt — 20 years old, a tall, astonishingly handsome Hungarian, one of the most commanding and fascinating personalities that has ever lived. Hearing Paganini, Liszt decided to do the same thing on the piano, and thereafter no pianist ever practiced as he practiced.

Robert Schumann, a boy of 12, was there and in his ardor to become a technical prodigy like that, on the piano, he permanently injured his fourth finger so that he had to become a composer and not a performer.

And Ole Bull, a 20-year-old Norwegian, strong, tall, beautiful, yellow-haired, was at the Paganini concert. He had had a few violin lessons as a boy and was self-taught. He was then studying law. Hearing Paganini he decided to be a violinist and to develop a prodigious technique.

When Paganini went to London wild stories preceded him — that he was a political victim who had been 20 years in a dungeon where he played all day long on an old broken violin with one string and thus got his wonderful mechanical dexterity. He could not walk the streets without being mobbed. In 1834 Berlioz composed for him his beautiful symphony, *Harold in Italy,* and this was the zenith of his fame and greatness. But his health, long since ruined by the ten-hour practicing, declined rapidly: tuberculosis. After much suffering he died in Nice in 1840.

He left a huge fortune and bequeathed one of his violins, a fine Joseph Guarnerius, to the city of Genoa. That is now one of its vaunted treasures.

Paganini's *cantabile* passages moved his audiences to tears, while his *tours de force* were so astonishing that a Viennese amateur publicly announced that he had seen the devil assisting him. He inaugurated an epoch — the first to show what could be done by technique. A genius, and his ghost will hover around the concert on Wednesday, if there are ghosts — and there certainly are — his tall, emaciated, gaunt figure and long black hair, his feverish, desperate, lovely, romantic, crystal music.

— 1947

# XII

This week is the Bach Festival (three concerts for 50 cents at Northrop Auditorium) and Friday at 8 o'clock the learned, impassioned, endearing Dr. Donald Ferguson will conduct the *Magnificat* and some of the *B Minor Mass.* For him another year of violent, tireless work has gone by, and all out of pure love.

These Bach people are very peculiar people. Every Monday night all year they go over to the University to practice, about a hundred of them —lawyers, housewives, bankers, druggists, students, society girls, Quaker conscientious objectors (in a state of scientific starvation for Dr. Ancel Keys). Dr. Ferguson in his shirt sleeves, his face haggard with beatific fatigue and enthusiasm, leads their singing with wild, happy, jerking, imploring violence. His shirt is soaking wet. In the excitement he shouts "Softer!" — and all the Bach people laugh and flash grins at him and each other, and sing it again.

Dr. Ferguson lives on Penn Avenue two blocks from Lake Harriet. He was born in

Wisconsin and there was a piano in the house and a brother could play a violin a little — "and you know how people who can do that like to get together," he says. He liked to play by ear and sing and improvise "and was always doing that."

Then he went to the University of Wisconsin, "where there was a French teacher, a man who knew almost everything —all languages, all literature, all art. . . " This wonderful man fired him and everybody so much they could see across the world and through Time, over all the punk music around them to the greatest geniuses who have walked this earth, like Bach, who could carry eleven tunes in his head at once, they say, weaving them in and out with such originality, nobility, variety, the world had never known the like.

So he began taking piano lessons and after the University he contrived to go to England for three years, studied with Michael Hambourg. Then in Minneapolis he taught in conservatories. Then Carlyle Scott needed someone to help him in the University music department. It was 1913.

Well, we don't half know him here or appreciate him, a distinguished man known in Europe with respect and gratitude. When I say,

"You have so much intellectual prowess, too, besides the music — " he flops in his chair indignantly and says "Oh bosh!" and then gives a radiant smile. But it is true. He wrote a preeminent book, *The History of Music.* When I asked how his book was received — "Well, that darned book . . . " and he shook his head with wonder. "Sir Granville Bantock —" "Who's that?" "The English composer. He sent me the Sunday London Observer, a very serious paper, you know, and my gosh, a whole darned page of it was about that book . . . Gee whiz . . ."

I said, "Your Bach Festival should become like the great one in Bethlehem, Pennsylvania. The greatest critics go to it." "Oh, our chorus are amateurs, amateurs. But it is truly wonderful how they have stood by for 13 years, many of them." And they "sing until our hearts melt within us" — as the Moravian Brethren said who came to Bethlehem from Germany and Bohemia in 1749, Hussites of long ago, a serious noble sect who believed that music is the best ladder for the soul to climb on. And Bach's music, the greatest of all.

A person who cannot feel music very much asked a person who loves music just what her experience is when she hears it. She tried to describe it. "It's like this. Say that you

want to express a thought like this: 'To believe
in God gives one a satisfying sense of security.'
Well that is straight prose and conveys the idea.

"But in poetry you'd say: 'The Lord
is my refuge and my fortress. His truth shall be
my sword and buckler.' That heightens your
comprehension more than the prose. It breaks
through the words, even uses the wrong words
and thereby comes closer to the true, inexpres-
sible, inward experience.

"But great music — Bach — raises this
comprehending aliveness to the Nth power. In
the *St. Matthew Passion* (Bach wrote the music
to the words of the Gospel of Matthew), when
they sing the words 'Jesus wept,' then you know
as you cannot possibly know in prose or in
poetry all that it means, what really happened,
the terrible pathos, significance, that someone
like Jesus could cry."

— 1942

# XIII

Saturday evening I went to a chamber music concert at the Walker Art Center: the Juilliard Quartet, all very young men with scholarly spectacles and tossed forelocks, playing Bartok. He is a famous living Hungarian composer. Every seat was taken and there were the most cultivated and eager and artistic people in town. There was Mr. Dorati, the conductor of the Minneapolis Symphony, John Sherman, the music critic, and Jane Sherman (John Sherman's wife and critic), Gerard Samuel, who conducts the Twilight Concerts, young professors in the English department, highbrow young wives with fancy earrings.

First they played a Bartok piece that was composed thirty years ago, then one composed recently and then one from the middle years. Well, every intelligent, attractive face in the audience took on a concentrated and intense look, and at intermission we strolled about and ejaculated: "Isn't it lovely? . . . Original! . . . Oh isn't it fun?"

But not me. I not only do not like any of it but feel tortured by the incoherent, jerky, inexplicable, truncated sounds. Sometimes it is like the buzzing of iron mosquitos and sometimes like the earsplitting shrieks of a streetcar coming around a corner on ungreased tracks.

And I thought to myself: "It is so strange that all music in the past, going back as far as Palestrina, or even to the ancient Greeks, may sound strange sometimes, but it is always pretty and beneficent, too."

But this modern music — Bartok, Schoenberg, Hindemith —is pure nerve-jerking pain. It makes me feel as though I were one of those *pate-de-fois* geese whose webbed feet are nailed to the floor and who is being forcibly fed to enlarge its liver.

But when I say things like this to those elect and wonderful people in the audience they all look upset. "Oh, really? . . . . Didn't you hear in that second piece some quite nice sounds —just for a minute? Why I did! Why I liked that part, I really did!"

Well, how to account for it? The Machine Age I suppose. It is Science not Beauty. They tell me the music is a marvel of complexity and vibrations and interwoven mathematics. "If you only knew musical composition!" I am sure of it! It must be wonderful like Dr. Athelstan Spilhaus's invention, the bathythermograph, that measures temperatures at various levels of sea water. But there is no beauty in it or human communication. And on the subject of the sea, or, that is to say, any human communication about the sea, give me Keats or Grieg and not the bathythermograph.

And even the great Mitropoulos told me that if you listened often enough you would get to like such music. Nope. I've tried that. It gets worse. And when friends say to me that they did not like such music at first but they do now after trying very, very hard and again and again and again, I say to them: "Well who knows? Maybe you have now acquired a perverted taste, like a man who forces himself to eat indigestible pickles for such a long time that at last he gets a craving for only indigestible pickles."

Well, as the great Russian writer Chekhov said, "Lord, do not allow me to condemn or speak of what I do not know or understand."

— 1956

# XIV

Marian Anderson, who comes to town today, has a short fierce nose in profile, the cheekbones slanting up in wild vigor like those sculptured young queens of the pharoahs at the Art Institute. Her father (who sold ice and fuel) died. Her mother (she had been a school teacher) went out washing and cleaning by the day. There were three little girls.

They went to the Union Baptist Church. Marian sang in the choir at 6 — about the size of a fly. From thenceforth this choir became her fun and her life. If the bass soloist didn't come — "Oh, Marian can sing it. . ." And if her voice now goes as high as the sky and as deep as the abyss — "two voices" they call it— it came from singing all the parts of any anthem. It would have injured any other voice. Not hers.

The church members started a fund "for Marian" with nickels and dimes and humble little benefits. It got to be 126 dollars. Then Roland Hayes happened to sing in the little church. He saw what she was. He found a teacher for her — Giuseppi Boghetti. When she was 20, Boghetti entered her in a singing contest. The winner was to sing with the New York Philharmonic — but Boghetti didn't tell her, he didn't want to scare her. He said to her that August day, when the judges looked so wan, so bored: "Even if you hear the gong, go on — so they can hear the trill at the end."

She won. She sang with the Philharmonic. It looked very easy. But for the next five years she was utterly blocked. Promises were mysteriously broken. A New York manager put her under contract, but nothing happened. And that's why she went abroad for eight years. She would go to Scandinavia for six concerts and stay for 75. She sold out the Paris Opera House. She visited Sibelius and after she sang for him he told the servant not to bring coffee — "Champagne!" he cried. "The roof of my house is too low for you."

The climax came in America, in 1939. She gave a free concert in Washington, and 75,000 people sat on the lawn, the President and the Cabinet and other great among the throng. She sang "My Country 'Tis of Thee" and "America" and "Nobody Know the Trouble I've Seen" under the immense, towering statue of Lincoln looking down, and he seemed to be thinking and thinking.

When I first heard her she wore a white dress with muffs of white fur around her wrists, and that was just right —wild, like nature and lynxes and jaguars in the green jungle, and pure, classical, tranquil like art." She sang Monteverdi and Handel. She sang "I'm a Long, Long Way from Home." And indeed she was, singing to thousands of prosperous white people who have had everything from the start.

— 1945

# XV

There was a dazzling concert at Hamline College, in that red stone castle with the spindly tower. The concert room is so charming and small — it curves all around the tiny stage. And so does a delicate wooden balcony. The audience can almost reach down and pat the musicians gratefully.

It was free. And seven pre-eminent musicians took part, five of them world-famous: Mitropoulos, Ernst Krenek, Joanna and Nikolai Graudan and Victor Babin.

Say that Grieg were exiled and Nina Grieg, Schumann, Joachim, Cesar Franck, etc. — that driven out of Europe they found an obscure livelihood here, nobody knowing much about it, and say they began to blow on the spark of living music to keep it alive — well, that is how it is.

First Ernst Krenek (he teaches at Hamline) described the music we were about to hear. It was "modern" music. They would expound it for us. It is that music we rage against (when we pay to hear it), throwing ourselves around in our seats like a horse in a shell-hole. As for Mr. Krenek (solid, steady, blue-eyed, the son of a Czech officer in the old Austrian army), his operas were performed all over Europe. Then he foreswore the old way of composing for "modern" music. They have played his music at the Symphony and I didn't like it (my fault, my limitation) and jeered for a while until I discovered that people who really know something —Mitropoulos, the Graudans — say that it is excellent, important.

Now Mrs. Briggs played piano pieces by Roger Sessions (a leading American composer who teaches at Princeton). And I thought they were beautiful, though I had to keep my mind pried open in a humble, effortful way. You see in listening to new music there is a frustration. It is because your mind cannot pour along it freely as when you hear Beethoven's Fifth Symphony or the "Swanee River." You are checked, blocked, the tune never goes where you think it will. Fatigue comes then and you give up trying. And probably go home saying: "Terrible! Like streetcars screeching as they go around a curve." But it isn't so.

Then Mme. Duschak (slim, black-browed, utterly charming) sang Charles Ives'

songs and Mitropoulos (wearing round glasses
on his handsome Dantesque nose) played the
piano for her. The songs were certainly queer.
But I wouldn't allow my Philistine self to
flounce off indignantly. I pinned all my under-
standing on each note.

The first one, "Summer ended, Har-
vest o'er," seemed pretty bad. The singer's
voice had to go now high, now low, see-sawed
from ceiling to basement, as though the composer had a devil of a time being original.

But then came a song written to the
words of Keats: "The Sick Eagle."

> "The spirit is too weak . . .
> Mortality weighs . . . tells me I must die
> Like a sick eagle, looking towards the sky."

I liked that. It was astounding how
that expressed what Keats meant. And was:
a sick eagle. And Mme. Duschak was a sick
eagle when she sang it. And Mitropoulos —
he was a sick eagle, too. You felt like a sick
eagle yourself, and how all of us are sick eagles,
our souls high in hope but sick and fainting
along the ground . . . with a touch of nausea,
indigestion.

Krenek played his own sonata, Mitropoulos turning the pages, sometimes radiantly

smiling as if to say: "Fine . . . How good it is
along here!"

And at the end Mr. and Mrs. Graudan
played a sonata by Victor Babin, a famous
Russian pianist. "The first time anywhere,"
said the program. And I could follow it with
easy eagerness. It was beautiful. (So was the
Krenek sonata, but I couldn't follow the "line"
of it — not that first time.)

While we were applauding, the Graudans were searching the audience with their
eyes. Where was he? "Come up! Come up!"
they wig-wagged to him. It was Babin himself. And Mrs. Graudan with her dauntless,
lovely air  went down the steps to lead him
by the hand  —an immense young man with
a fur cap of hair like a Yale boy.

Mr. Krenek said that if we like the
concerts there will be more. And it was free.
And I keep thinking how so much of musicians' work is free, how the infinitesimal perfection of this evening's music, the faintest
plucked thirty-second note, had been sought,
practiced for the ten-thousandth time. "He
whose face has no light in it shall never become a star."

— 1943

# XVI

For the next three months, from February until June, I wrote every day some news for the radio, and I did it very well and made some money. But toward summer I felt low-spirited and quite downhearted for a reason that I cannot tell about. And when this is so, I have this longing to go far away, to be disconnected from any base, and to move through some vast distance, endless space — perhaps on the Trans-Siberian railroad.

Anne in New York was taking piano lessons from Seroff, whom she considered an extraordinary pianist, a genius, a wonderful person. She thought it would be good for Seroff and all of us if he came out here for the summer and lived in our house and we all took lessons. And I thought: "Fine. If I can't go to Siberia, why, Siberia and the Caucasus and Vienna and Paris can come here in the person of Seroff. And that will be the next best thing."

Harriet, Margaret, Dorothy Lewis and I and all the children took lessons. There was a Steinway concert piano as long as a locomotive in the sitting room, and another one for playing double pianos; and our old family piano was hoisted upstairs in my room so that music, the sound of practicing, now came floating out of all four houses, and even from the upstairs windows, all day long.

Seroff was Russian, young and black-haired with small slant eyes and a cowlick in his eyebrows and darkly, tragically handsome, especially when he was gloomy and contemptuous. But although cold and haughty to strangers, he was funny, twinkly, humble, offhand and affectionate to everyone he knew well. In his short Tyrolean pants and red suspenders and loose dark-blue linen shirt, he would go slapping up and downstairs in his slippers, and in and out of the kitchen and down to sit in the lake, with the water to his waist, while he read the newspaper. For as the winter had been cold, the summer was the hottest one there had ever been. "Today you are Papa Bach," I would say to Seroff, when he was so *gemutlich* and entertaining and wanting company and (I think) almost afraid to be alone.

But in giving lessons he was fierce and contemptuous — or, it may have been, just to me. He was terribly scornful of the measliness

of effort that he would get out of us. Of course
I had to astonish him. I wasn't going to have
*that.* I worked like the devil with my very
limited knowledge and technique.

"All right, if you think you're so much,"
he would say to me, when several people were
at Rolf's house, "play your piece for them.
The Moussorgsky."

"Sure I will. You bet your life." And
I would go to the piano and tackle it, hammer
away as best I could.

"All right, Indian, if you think you're
such a pirate. Play the Schumann Fantasia."

"O. K."

The first day he came he seized upon
a word I use very much: "namby-pamby."
Thereafter he said that about almost everybody.
"Ahk! *she* play the Appassionata? Never! too
pansy-wamsy!" Or if you said that you have
been practicing for three and a half hours:
"Practicing! I heard you. You were just lulla-
bying yourself!" And at a lesson, when you
started to play for him, a Mozart concerto, say,
he shouted and tore your hands from the keys.
"*No!*" And then he would shriek. "Put something into it! When a Russian makes love they
*crush the bones!*"

That was a lovely summer. Seroff

would practice for four or five hours every morning, such wonderful music, like Beethoven's greatest sonata, Op. 111. And you cannot imagine what an effect that has on you, to hear that music again and again and again, as though you were absorbing some kind of blessed, blessed mysterious sunlight. One Sunday morning Sandra consented to pose for us, so out under the elm trees, we all drew her with pastels — Anne and Ken and Elsa, too, for they were home then. And Seroff's music came floating out of the sitting room window. That was one of the best days of my life: that unspeakably beautiful music floating about us and touching us all with gold, and the summer day, and all those nice people. And my drawing of Sandra was just wonderful.

(From Brenda Ueland's autobiography *Me.*)

— 1939

# XVII

This is not a retraction. It is a confession. I don't think I should have said about Herman Melville's poem set to Ernst Krenek's music that it was "skillful, hideous and interesting." I thought as I wrote it, "How clever I am, how skylarking!" But my conscience began chewing and gnawing at me in the middle of the night, and today, and won't desist. It was the word "hideous." I should have put instead the adjective "disturbing." And Krenek's music fitted the poems like skin, and the young choir was just lovely, just perfection. "Hideous" was only a fraction of what was true about the music. It was at the same time dramatic, mysterious, fantastical, ingenious, and so on.

"Why then did you say 'hideous?' " I ask myself, and answer:

"I try to like Mr. Krenek's music and cannot. I cannot participate in it for two seconds on end. I can't sing it, sail along in it. Then, in haste and exasperation, I say 'hideous.' "

"Well, what of it then? If you think so, say so."

"Yes," my conscience answers. "Say

it with your voice but not in print. In print
you are saying it to 75,000 people, our newspaper's circulation, while one's voice says it to
two or three. And you can see by their expression, or sleepiness, or joking smile that 'hideous'
is only part of what you mean."

But all this is why writing is harder
than talking. If you have a conscience you
must be 75,000 times more careful not to give
a wrong, untrue impression than when you say
it with your voice. Because if 75,000 get the
wrong impression that is like telling 75,000
lies.

And to write of music or people or
politics is all right only if you labor to give the
whole story, the whole essential good-or-bad
of it, the 89 percent good and the 11 percent
bad. And it's hard work. And writing a col-
umn a day is too hurried for complete, serious
thought about some things.

And another reason your conscience as
a writer must be membrane-thin: the writer
has such un unfair advantage. He can lay about
him with adjectives and his conceited opinions
and give 75,000 wrong impressions by one
paragraph, while the poor victim he wounds
(and prejudices 75,000 minds against) cannot
answer back to those 75,000. The poor victim

can only write one letter, perhaps telling the critic he's an idiot.

So writing can be like hunting: you kill one harmless and perfect creature at a great safe distance without the slightest danger to yourself.

— 1944

**CREDITS**:

Editors:  Bruce Carlson
         Carl Johnson

Production Assistance:
         Sharon Carlson

Cover Photograph:
         Minnesota Historical Society